HUMAN BODY

KINGFISHER
NEW YORK

KINGFISHER
LONDON & NEW YORK

Text and design copyright © Toucan Books Ltd. 2011
Based on an original concept by Toucan Books Ltd.
Illustrations copyright © Simon Basher 2011

Published in the United States by Kingfisher,
175 Fifth Ave., New York, NY 10010
Kingfisher is an imprint of Macmillan Children's Books, London.
All rights reserved.

Consultant: Dougal Hargreaves

Designed and created by Basher www.basherbooks.com
Text written by Dan Green

Dedicated to Jean and Colette Rollet

Distributed in the U.S. and Canada by Macmillan, 175 Fifth Ave.,
New York, NY 10010

Library of Congress Cataloging-in-Publication data has been applied for.

ISBN: 978-0-7534-6501-1

Kingfisher books are available for special promotions and premiums.
For details contact: Special Markets Department, Macmillan,
175 Fifth Ave., New York, NY 10010.

For more information, please visit www.kingfisherbooks.com

Printed in China
9 8 7 6 5 4 3
3TR/0911/WKT/UNTD/140MA

CONTENTS

Introduction
Human Body

Your body is a most amazing machine. It is armed with toollike hands, propelled by two legs, and governed by a brain capable of independent thought (well, sometimes), speech, and problem solving. Supertough on the outside—think skin, hair, nails—your insides comprise all the delicate organs and impressively sophisticated body systems that keep you in perfect shape.

Though you are undoubtedly gorgeous to look at, most of your best parts are hidden from view. Anatomy whiz Andreas Vesalius (1514–1564) decided to take a look for himself. It was a grisly job that involved dissecting a few cadavers (dead bodies to you) and rummaging around inside. He stuck it out, though, making detailed drawings, and discovered that all sorts of accepted "facts" about the human body were actually wrong. For example, he dispelled the myth that women have one rib more than men. He also found that the liver had just two lobes and not five, as suspected. Thanks to him, we know so much more about our bodies and the mind-blowing life beneath our skin. Well, come on, let's get inside . . .

Andreas Vesalius

Man and Woman

* Adult members of the species *Homo sapiens sapiens*
* The same kind of living thing, but each with subtle differences
* Like other mammal females, Woman gives birth to live young

Make way, the humans are coming! We are a daring duo, powerful beasts, striding out on two legs. We are the same animal but exist as either Man or Woman. And when we get together, sparks really fly—for together we make Baby.

Man is the taller, more muscular variety. He wears his sex organs on the outside, and his teenage body changes are fueled by the hormone testosterone. Woman's sex organs are tucked away inside her body so that she can nurture Baby for nine months. The female hormone estrogen triggers a different set of body changes that allow her to do this. Our gender is determined by two chromosomes called "X" and "Y"—two Xs for a female, and an X and a Y for a male. Only Man carries a Y, so it's up to him as to which mini version of us you get to be!

● Tallest human: Robert Wadlow (8.92 ft., or 2.72m)
● Oldest human: Jeanne Calment (122 years and 164 days; 1875–1997)
● Average weight: Man, 168–183 lb. (76–83kg); Woman, 119–141 lb. (54–64kg)

Man and Woman

Baby

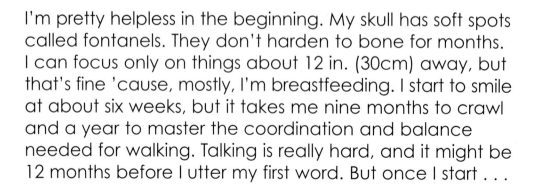

- ☀ This young imp is the offspring of Man and Woman
- ☀ Born after about 40 weeks' gestation in Woman's body
- ☀ Infant babies drink milk produced by their mothers

I am the pinnacle of creation. Life's greatest little trick. I start out as one unimaginably small cell, when Man's sperm combines with Woman's egg: the moment of fertilization. Nine months later, I pop out—that big-headed, chubby, wailing, feeding, and pooping machine you just can't help loving! Ahh. Coochy coo!

I'm pretty helpless in the beginning. My skull has soft spots called fontanels. They don't harden to bone for months. I can focus only on things about 12 in. (30cm) away, but that's fine 'cause, mostly, I'm breastfeeding. I start to smile at about six weeks, but it takes me nine months to crawl and a year to master the coordination and balance needed for walking. Talking is really hard, and it might be 12 months before I utter my first word. But once I start . . .

- ● Normal duration of pregnancy: 35–40 weeks
- ● Average weight at birth: 7.1 lb. (3.2kg)
- ● Average length at birth: 14–20 in. (35.6–50.8cm)

Baby

CHAPTER 1
Body Building Blocks

It all starts with these tiny tots. Before you became a running, jumping, eating, breathing, speaking, bad-smell-making all-around hero, you were an insignificant microdot of cells. Here, then, for your delight and entertainment, are the microscopic marvels that make up wonderful you! It all starts with Cell, whose eight guises make up Body Tissue. Then you have your bone builders, your muscle makers, your delivery men, your defense team, and your sense centers. Don't miss this once-in-a-lifetime chance to lift the lid on your body and see what goes on inside. Go on—take a peek, if you dare!

Cell

DNA

Gene

Mitochondrion

Protein

Stem Cell

Sperm

Egg

Nerve Cell

Red Blood Cell

White
Blood Cells

Osteoblast

Body Tissue

Cell
■Body Building Blocks

- ☀ A tiny unit of living matter inside a membrane
- ☀ It's all systems go in this chemical factory that runs your body
- ☀ Eight basic types of specialist cells make up the human body

All great things come in small packages, and I'm no exception. I am *the* definitive building block. Everything that happens in your body happens because of me. I might be small, but I'm no lightweight, I can assure you!

Put me under the microscope and you'll see what I mean. Inside my cool plasma membrane, I'm busy working with all sorts of chemicals to make everything you need to keep your body functioning. Dig a little deeper and you'll find my nucleus. This limited-access area is my control center and the home of your genius gene-giving DNA.

I don't like to work alone, though. It takes millions of me to make up your whole body. I divide to make copies of myself, so there are always enough of me to go around.

- ● Average size: 0.0004–0.0012 in. (0.01–0.03 mm)
- ● Number of cells in a fertilized egg: 1
- ● Number of cells in a human body: 50 trillion to 100 trillion

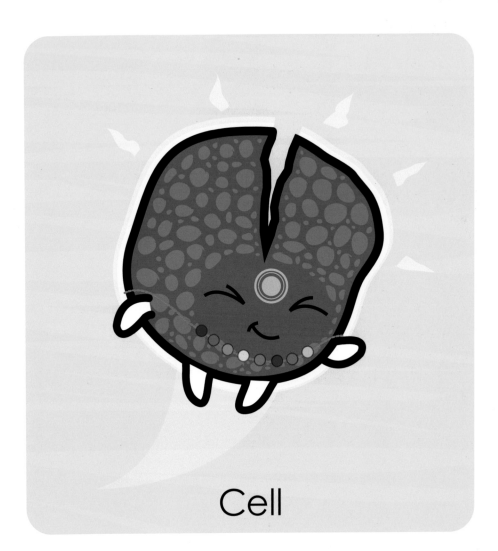

Cell

DNA
Body Building Blocks

* Found in almost every cell of your body
* Can be used to identify an individual, just like a fingerprint
* Only identical twins have *exactly* the same DNA

It's hard not to feel important when your name is Deoxyribonucleic Acid, and—dare I say it—I am a rather special chemical compound. You see, I hold the key to the secret of life!

I am a learned fellow known as a double helix. My two sleek strands are chemically linked together like a ladder and spiraled like a corkscrew. My bases (the ladder rungs) are made from just four substances, but in long sequences, they form a complex code that tells your body how to work. My home is Cell's nucleus, where 46 strips of me are arranged in 23 pairs called chromosomes. I'm like a blueprint for who you are. And whenever Cell divides, I make an exact copy of myself so that all your cells carry the same code. Face it—without me, you wouldn't be you.

* Number of different chromosomes in the body: 46 (in 23 pairs)
* Number of bases in a chromosome: 50 million to 280 million
* DNA discoverer: Friedrich Miescher (1869)

DNA

Gene
Body Building Blocks

* A small portion of DNA on a chromosome
* Genes tell the body how to build or operate its parts
* Your genes are passed on to you from both parents

Are you clumsy, like your dad? Tone deaf, like your mom? Blame little old me. I'm a how-to guide for the human body—the instructions for making, running, and maintaining body parts. I'm crucial to your appearance and natural abilities because your body's cells use me to build parts such as your brain, skin, hair, eyes, and nose. I come in pairs—one set from Mom and one from Dad.

I'm unbelievably tiny: inside Cell's nucleus are 46 strands of DNA, tightly curled up. These are called chromosomes. Straighten them all out and they'd stretch almost 10 ft. (3m) and contain about 50,000 of me! Small sequences of DNA signal the end of one gene and the start of another so that a chromosome can be understood—just as a capital letter and a period give sense to sentences. Gene-ius!

● Genetic similarity between humans: 99.998%
● Genetic similarity between a human and a mouse: 92%
● Number of genes on a chromosome: up to 3,000

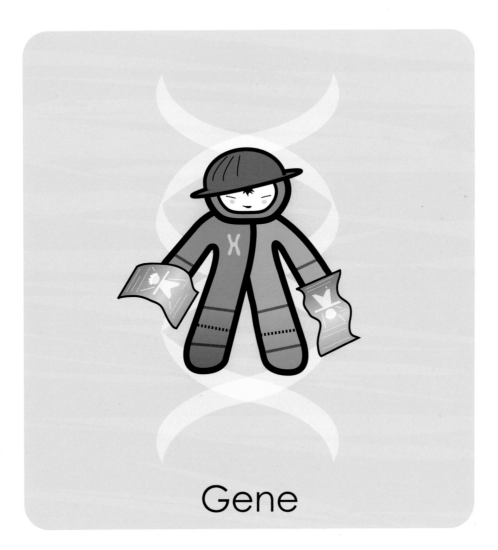

Gene

Mitochondrion
Body Building Blocks

- The pocket rocket—the power supply inside your cells
- A torpedo-shaped hot rod that dismantles cells when they die
- DNA in mitochondria is passed on through your mother

Fast and furious, I'm the little guy who generates Cell's power. And it's no mean feat! I whiz around (there are millions of us) making a fuel called ATP. It's full of life-giving energy and is ready whenever Cell needs some juice. The more she wants, the more we make. And when demand threatens to exceed supply, we simply divide and multiply to increase our output.

Mitochondrion

- Size: 0.00002–0.0004 in. (0.0005–0.01mm)
- Number of genes: 37
- ATP production: 5 million per second

Protein

Body Building Blocks

* Long chains of amino acids arranged in fixed sequences
* Groups of chemicals that include enzymes and blood cells
* Protein chains have shapes that relate to their function

Protein

I'm a busybody, a doer, a jack-of-all-trades. My funky, chainlike form gets made inside your cells. It's built from amino acids that are absorbed from food and arranged in different sequences. You'll find me hanging around in every corner of your body. And, boy, am I eager, just waiting for an opportunity to help digest your food, carry oxygen to your cells, and keep you healthy.

● Number of amino acids in the body: 20
● Keratin: a protein found in skin, hair, and nails
● Elastin: a protein found in skin and arteries

Stem Cell
Body Building Blocks

- A cell with fantastic morphing potential
- Found in embryos, bone marrow, the liver, and the brain
- Could be used for growing replacement body parts

I am the cell with infinite potential, the Special One—have no doubt! There's no other cell quite like me, because I can become any type of cell that takes my fancy. My cellular cousins start and end life as specialists—in the brain or skin, for example—but me, I'm a mighty morpher.

I'm not just boasting! My unique shape-shifting talents make me incredibly valuable. Just think about it: because I can divide to become anything from kidney cells to muscle or heart cells, I could one day be used to create custom-made organs for transplants. So how do I do it? Well, I multiply, just like Cell does. But when I split, each new cell gets to choose whether to stay the same or become something different. Mmm, let's see . . . Nerve Cell? Nah . . . Muscle Cell . . . ? Maybe . . .

- Number of different types of cell that a stem cell can become: 220
- Most common stem cells: located in three- to five-day-old embryo
- Adult stem cells: found mostly in bone marrow and skin

Stem Cell

Sperm
Body Building Blocks

* One of millions that race to fertilize an egg
* This swimming champ carries only a half set of DNA
* Carries an X or a Y chromosome to decide the sex of a baby

On your mark. Get set. Go! I'm called a spermatozoon, but I prefer spermatozoom because I'm one speedy kind of guy. Lovely Egg and I make new life.

I'm a little guy with a big job, and my life is brief but glorious. Starting from the testes, a man's sperm factory, I travel upstream toward the penis. I pick up fluids as I pass the prostate gland, and these give me fuel for my journey. If everything goes "swimmingly," I enter the female body and whip my long tail for the hour's swim to my eggy destination. Sounds easy? Are you kidding? It's a real challenge. First, I have to reach Egg before she gets too old (believe me, it's a small window). Second, I have to race against several million of my own kind. There's no denying it—you've gotta be brave!

* Swimming speed: 0.04–0.12 in. (1–3mm) per minute
* Number of sperm produced per day: 50 million to 500 million
* Length of a sperm head: 0.002 in. (0.05mm)

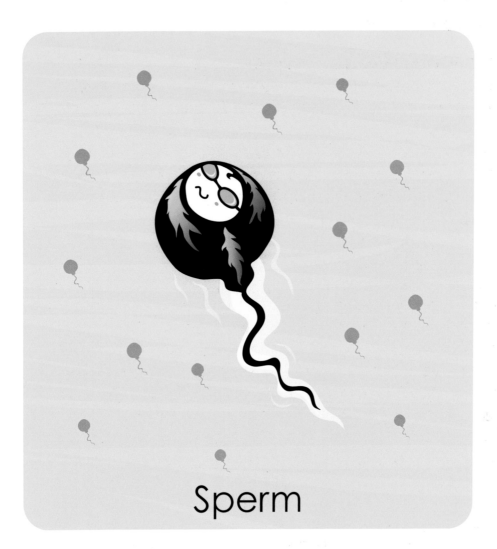

Sperm

Egg
Body Building Blocks

* The largest cell made by the human body
* A woman releases only 400 of these cells in a lifetime
* The female sex cell—its scientific name is ovum

Graceful and gorgeous, I ripen in a woman's ovary just once a month. Like a tiny bubble, I float dreamily down the fallopian tube, hoping that speedy Sperm is on his way to find me.

I'm an easy target—85,000 times larger than Sperm in terms of volume—so his chances of finding me should be pretty high. Each of us has a half set of DNA, and if Sperm makes it, these fuse to create a brand-new being. Then, deep within the protection of the uterus, I start to grow into Baby. It's awesome, but there is a catch; we simply don't have much time. Within just 24 hours of starting my journey, I will have grown too old for that all-important meeting. And if Sperm doesn't show up? I exit, during a woman's monthly period, so that another Egg can try in four weeks.

● Life span of an egg after release: 24 hours
● Diameter of fertilized egg: 0.006 in. (0.15mm)
● Time a fertilized egg takes to grow into a baby: 35–40 weeks

Egg

Nerve Cell
Body Building Blocks

* Your central nervous system acts on messages from your brain
* There are approximately 100 billion nerve cells in the brain
* Controls automatic functions, such as breathing and sweating

I am a real live wire, a special type of cell that passes messages from all parts of your body to your brain. I help you sense the world around you, move around, and feel pain. That's me—highly charged and ready for action.

You are, quite literally, one big bag of nerves. I'm joined together in long chains that connect you from head to toe. Each one of me has tiny threadlike extensions called fibers that make me extra touchy-feely. I'm like a superefficient network of shiny wires with electrical signals speeding along me like greased lightning!

Brain likes to order me around, but there are some things I control automatically—like regulating your body temperature—so you never have to think about them.

- Width of nerve fiber: 0.0004 in. (0.01mm)
- Strength of nerve signal: more than 30 millivolts (mV)
- Average nerve signal duration: 0.001 seconds

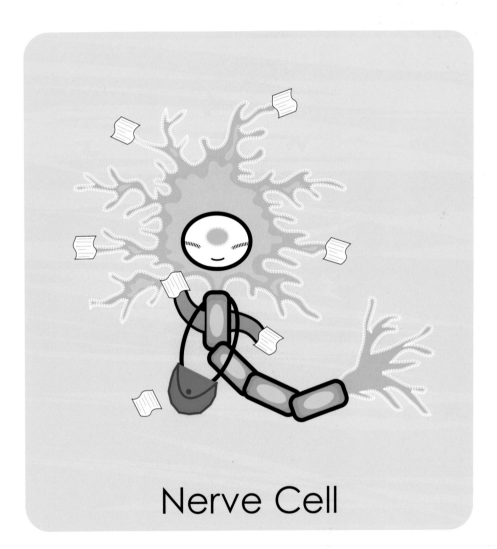

Nerve Cell

Red Blood Cell
Body Building Blocks

- A cell made in your bone marrow
- This rosy roustabout carries oxygen around your body
- One drop of blood contains 250 million of these guys

Forever young, I'm a specialist trained to bring life-giving oxygen to Cell. Duty calls me whenever and wherever I'm needed. Call me a doughnut if you like—I'm shaped like one, and with no genes of my own, I'm a simple kind of guy—but I perform a vital task.

Just one of me can carry a billion oxygen molecules! I use an iron-rich chemical called hemoglobin to pick up oxygen as I travel through the lungs with Blood. It's an exhausting task, and in about 120 days (and almost 600 blood-soaked miles, or 1,000km), I've just about had it.

No easy retirement for me, though. Liver breaks me down, and I get flushed out of the body in urine. My lovely red color becomes the yellow in your pee. What a washout!

- Average size: 0.0003 in. (0.007mm)
- Number of red blood cells in the body: 25 trillion
- Red blood cell discoverer: Jan Swammerdam (1658)

Red Blood Cell

White Blood Cells

Body Building Blocks

* Blood cells that form part of your immune system
* These guys go by the scientific name of leukocytes
* The little critters increase in number to fight off disease

Meet the White Blood Cell squad, an elite unit in your bloodstream. "To serve and protect" is our motto, and we live and die by it. Our mission? To seek and destroy.

Five of us operate in this tight outfit, each with his own jurisdiction. We roam your body looking for creeps and lowlifes who barge in uninvited. Bacteria, viruses, cancer cells—you name them, we're onto them. Neutrophil targets infections that invade through broken skin. Basophil triggers allergic-response chemicals. Eosinophil stalks parasites, and Monocyte mops up debris. Heading up the crew is Lymphocyte, AKA Captain Immunity. He kills off body cells gone bad and protects against future disease. Unlike most of the WBC squad, who last only hours or days, Lymphocyte can live for a few years.

● Proportion of WBCs in blood: 0.7%
● Number of WBCs in the body: 20–55 billion
● Breakdown: neutro. (62%), lympho. (27%), mono. (6%), eosino. (4%), baso. (1%)

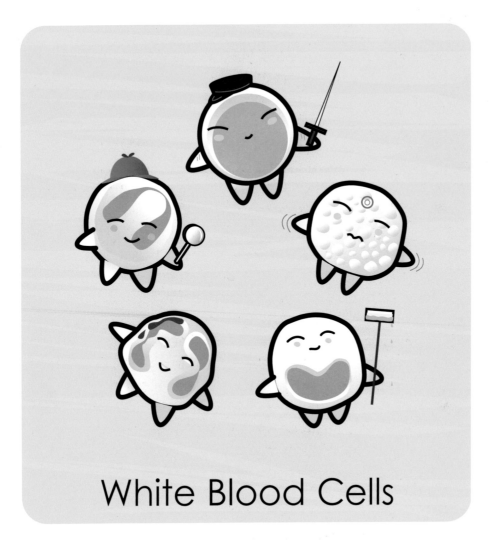

White Blood Cells

Osteoblast

Body Building Blocks

- Bone-making cell generated by stem cells in the bone marrow
- Your body uses this guy to fix broken bones
- This hard cell dies off in elderly people

A tough little hardhat, I am the foundation of the bone construction business. Without me and my pals, the whole industry would collapse (taking you with it). So if you've never heard of me before, you'd better bone up!

I lay down calcium phosphate, the rock-hard stuff that makes your skeleton. Some collagen goes into the mix, too. This keeps your bones a little flexible and makes them less brittle. Highly specialized, I make two types of bone. The first is spongy and forms a honeycomb mesh down Bone's center. It's packed with wobbly bone marrow. The second is compact—literally thousands of us huddled tightly together—and is used to make Bone's tough outer sheath. I'm always at it, constantly replacing the cells in your bones—never call me bone idle!

- Strongest bone in the body: thighbone (femur)
- Bone is four times lighter than steel
- About one-seventh of total body weight is bone

Osteoblast

Body Tissue
Body Building Blocks

* Made from layers of similar cells working together
* All the functional parts of your body are made from tissue
* Important tissues are bone, fat, collagen, muscle, and blood

I am the fabulously sloppy stuff that fills your holes and holds you together. When it comes to building your body, humdrum Cell may start the job, but it's definitely *me* who finishes it off. Honestly, she'd be nothing on her own!

I am the innard wizard! Call me smarmy, but I can't help it. I ooze class as I arrange Cell into different groups and layers to make all your gorgeously gloppy insides. Gristle, sinew, marrow, muscle, fat, and slippery membranes—these are all thanks to me and my meticulous organization. Even those self-satisfied, puffed-up complex organs like Heart, Kidney, and Skin are made simply by combining layers of my various, wonderfully unctuous functional units. Now that's what I call "organ"-ized!

● Types of tissue: connective, muscle, nervous, epithelial
● Connective tissue: bone, blood, and collagen
● Epithelial tissue: skin

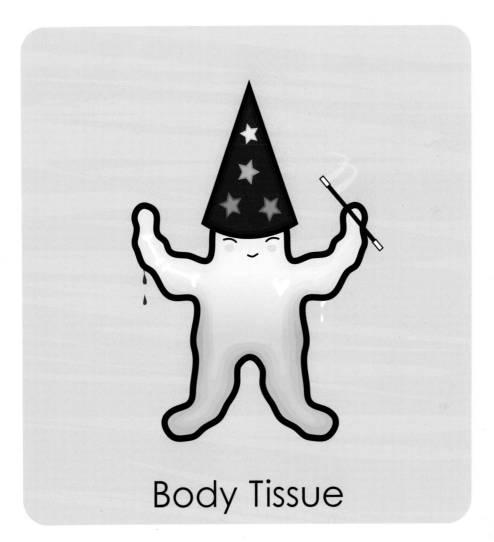

Body Tissue

CHAPTER 2
Musculoskeletal Meatheads

Let's have some respect for this upstanding crew! Without these fellows, you'd be a jellylike lump on the floor. They're the guys who give you shape, put steel into your body, and get you moving around. First, there's Bone, who makes up your skeleton. Spine and thick Skull are part of his setup, providing you with all that superstrength and protection. Then you've got Skeletal Muscle. Frankly, he's the one that sets it all in motion. He'd find it difficult without Cartilage, though, who ties your bones together at their creaking joints. But, hey, come on and meet this upright crowd—it'll be a "moving" experience!

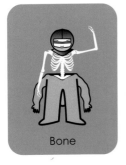

Bone

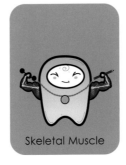

Skeletal Muscle

Cartilage

Skull

Spine

Bone

■ Musculoskeletal Meatheads

* ☀ This hard case forms your internal skeleton
* ☀ A living organ made up of different cells and supplied by blood
* ☀ Of the 206 bones in your body, 106 are in your hands and feet

Hard as they come, I'm your bodyguard, your knight in shining armor. As Skull, I protect your vulnerable brain, and as your ribs, I help shelter your heart and lungs.

I'm made of pretty stern stuff, from the longest bone in your thigh (femur) to the smallest bone in your ear (stapes). I form the complex framework on which you hang your organs. You use me like a set of levers to move your limbs around. Make no bones about it, without me, you'd be nothing more than a crumpled heap of flesh. You'd think I was dead, but I am very much alive, I can assure you. Ask Osteoblast, who does my maintenance. Osteoblasts are always making more of me to help you grow bigger, and they patch me up when I break. Here's something else: I can stick around for a thousand years without rotting.

* ● Weight of an adult skeleton: about 14% of total body weight
* ● Number of ribs in a human body: 24 (in 12 pairs)
* ● One in 200 people have one or two extra ribs

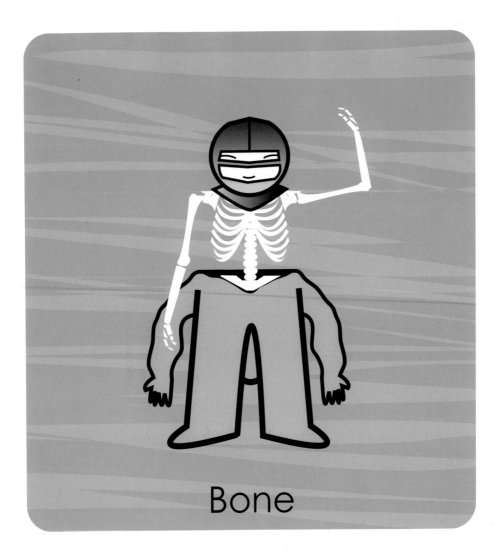

Bone

Skeletal Muscle
■ Musculoskeletal Meatheads

☀ A main body tissue, this meathead loves to move it
☀ Bundles of protein fibers, joined to the bones by tendons
☀ One of three muscle brothers (along with cardiac and smooth)

Pay no attention to gloating Bone—it's me that keeps you upright. I'm the muscle behind your every move, got it? The expressions "bone idle," "lazybones," and "bonehead" haven't come out of thin air—Bone is all talk and no action, and you heard it here first!

Just look at me. I'm a bulked-up, boisterous body builder that makes up about 40 percent of your body weight. I work hard, but my long ropy fibers can pull only in one direction, so I work in pairs. One bunch bends while the other bunch straightens. My length shortens as I pull, which is why I bulge when I tighten. I need to be big to support and move Bone around, but I can also make myself small for fine, controlled movements like writing or raising an eyebrow. Hey, I'm not a total meathead!

● Number of muscles in the human body: about 639
● Fastest muscle movements: those controlling the eye (200–400 milliseconds)
● Number of muscles used for walking: more than 200

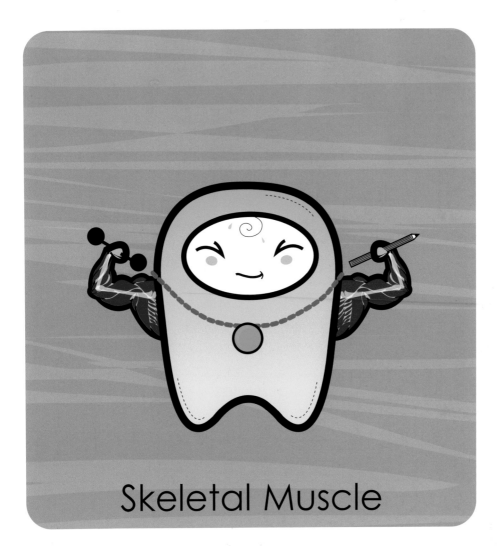

Skeletal Muscle

Cartilage

■ Musculoskeletal Meatheads

✳ One of the body's main connective tissues
✳ Less flexible than muscle but not as hard as bone
✳ Your nose and the outer parts of your ear are made of this

Hail the ultimate middleman, the mighty connector. Soft and pliable, I'm your flexible friend. I'll bend over backward to help you walk, twist, jump, sit, and dance.

Face it, you'd be as stiff as a board if you were made from hard-man Bone alone. He's so tough that he doesn't *do* bending. Something's gotta give, and that's where I come in. I'm the superhip linkster that connects ligaments and tendons to Bone. Ligaments join one bone to the next, while tendons attach the muscles. I also make flat disks to separate Spine's bony rings and stop them from battering and clattering against each other. All in all, it's me that keeps you hanging together as one superflexible mobile being . . . 'cause the knee bone's connected to the thighbone, the thighbone's connected to the hipbone . . .

● Elastic cartilage: found in the outer ear
● Fibrocartilage: found in intervertebral disks
● Hyaline cartilage: found in gristle

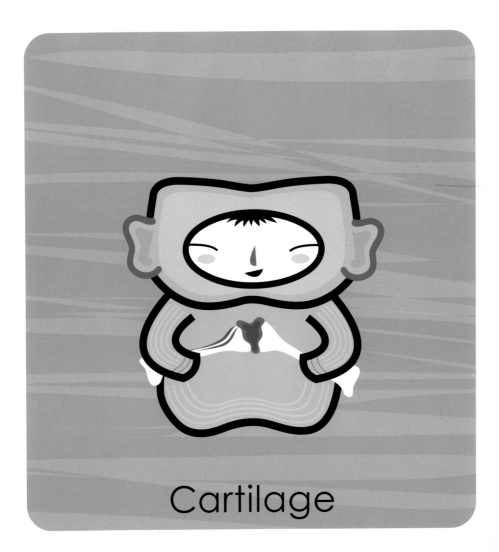

Cartilage

Skull

■ Musculoskeletal Meatheads

* A hardheaded collection of 22 fused bones
* This blockhead runs a protection racket for your brain
* Has cushioning layers of body tissue beneath the surface

Hey-hey—I'm a total braincase! I'm more of a bonehead than a brainiac, and yet I have this mentally important job! What were they thinking?

Actually, I'm a pretty sophisticated piece of equipment. My bony mask makes a good home for delicate sense organs—ears and eyes to you—and for your gnashers. It's also a blank canvas on which to pin your muscles and your facial features. Handy hinges operate your jawbone so that you can chew and chat to your heart's content. Eight of my bones are fused together to make your neurocranium. That's the superhard shell that saves soft Brain from knocks. I'm pretty tough but no match for concrete. So do me a favor and wear a helmet when you're out riding your bike. Unlike me, it's a no-brainer!

● Fontanels: soft spots on a baby's skull that make it flexible during birth
● Number of fontanels in a newborn baby's skull: 6
● Age at which all fontanels have closed: 2 years

Skull

Spine
■ Musculoskeletal Meatheads

✴ This straight-up character is the backbone of your body
✴ Your lower back, called the lumbar spine, carries most weight
✴ Often the cause of aches and pains in older adults

Call me proud and upright, even straight-laced, but I don't have a bone to pick. You see, you can thank me when you stand on your own two feet and hold your head up high.

Reach around to the middle of your back and you'll find my graceful line. I'm a stack of bony rings separated by disks of clever Cartilage. Without him, I'd be like a high-rise pile of greasy plates, wobbly and ready to tumble. Instead, I'm a tower of strength. At my very top are the axis and atlas bones that allow you to nod your head for "yes" and shake for "no." At my very bottom (and yours!) is the coccyx—your tailbone. Your ribs hook into me to provide protection for your body's soft organs. And right down my middle is a circular cavity that encloses your vital spinal cord. That takes some nerve! Get it?

● Name for each individual bone: vertebra (plural vertebrae)
● Number of vertebrae in a human spine: 33
● Number of vertebrae separated by disks: 24

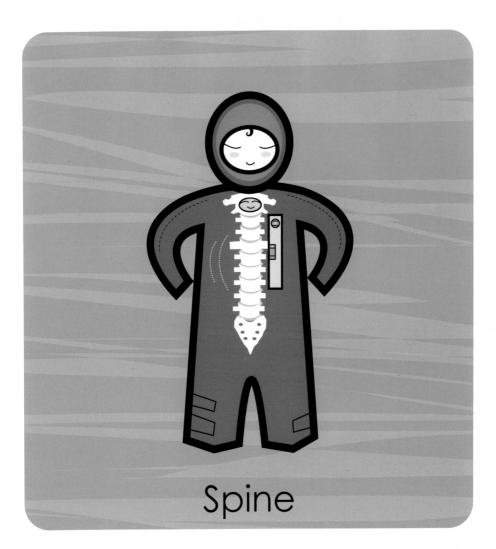

Spine

CHAPTER 3
Wheezing Windbags and Bloody Busybodies

Put your hands together for your circulatory system. Fronted by Heart and awash with Blood, this is an amazing, fully automatic butler service for your body. It supplies your body's cells with oxygen and fuel, repairs damage to the skin, protects against microscopic bacterial invasion, defends against disease, *and* carts away your cells' waste products and nasty toxins. Not bad, huh? But wait! Save some praise for those gasbags, Lungs, who control your respiratory system. They are in charge of getting oxygen and carbon dioxide out of your blood. It's the ultimate clean-up act—don't miss it!

Heart

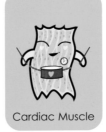

Cardiac Muscle

Blood

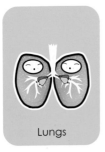

Lungs

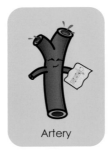

Artery

Capillary

Vein

Heart

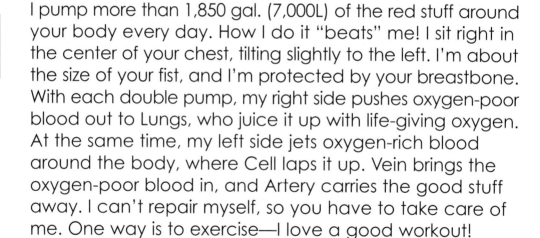

■ Wheezing Windbags and Bloody Busybodies

❋ A double-action pump that sends blood around your body
❋ Cardiac muscle keeps this bighearted guy pumping
❋ Cardiac arrest is when the heart suddenly loses its steady beat

Stop! Listen very carefully . . . That *lub-dub, lub-dub* you hear is me beating out the rhythm of your life. I'm the rootin'-tootin' lubba-lubba man, and I'm *all* heart!

I pump more than 1,850 gal. (7,000L) of the red stuff around your body every day. How I do it "beats" me! I sit right in the center of your chest, tilting slightly to the left. I'm about the size of your fist, and I'm protected by your breastbone. With each double pump, my right side pushes oxygen-poor blood out to Lungs, who juice it up with life-giving oxygen. At the same time, my left side jets oxygen-rich blood around the body, where Cell laps it up. Vein brings the oxygen-poor blood in, and Artery carries the good stuff away. I can't repair myself, so you have to take care of me. One way is to exercise—I love a good workout!

● Average weight of a human heart: male, 10.6 oz. (300g); female, 8.8 oz. (250g)
● Average adult heart rate: 60 beats per minute (at rest)
● Capacity of blood pumped: 1,900 gal. (7,200L) per day

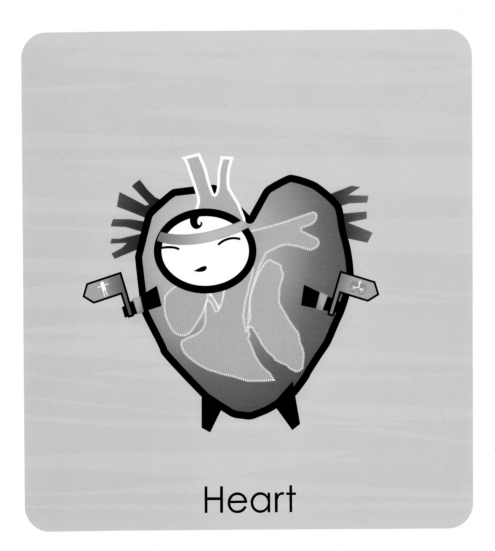

Heart

Cardiac Muscle

■ Wheezing Windbags and Bloody Busybodies

☀ A special type of muscle that powers the heart
☀ Beefy brother of skeletal muscle and smooth muscle
☀ Officially the hardest-working part of your body

Tick, tock, tick, tock. That's my mantra. I am what Heart is made of, the muscle that powers old lover boy's activity. Small but perfectly formed, I have just one job to do, and, believe me, I do it magnificently.

Always pumped up and ready for action, I work without taking a break to keep Blood on the move. You see, if Heart stops beating, Brain can survive only for a few minutes without the life-giving oxygen that Blood brings. And you know what that means . . . Ugh, it makes me *flutter* even to think about it!

In the pumping stakes, I'm second to none. Aided by a small knot of pacemaker cells, I beat a steady rhythm. So it's me that makes that old ticker tick (tock)!

● Scientific name: myocardium
● Cardiac muscle cells are called cardiomyocytes
● Frequency: 100,000 beats per day

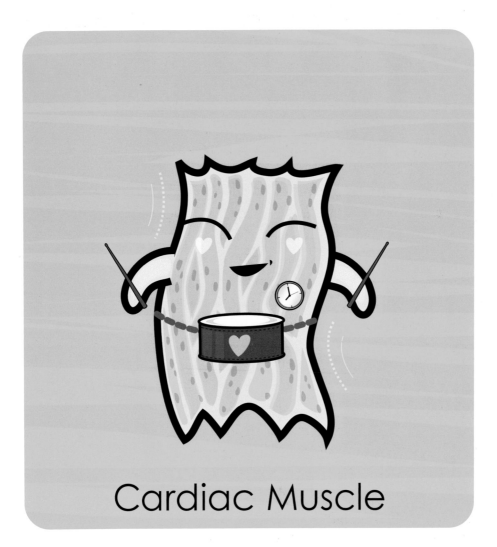

Cardiac Muscle

Blood

■ Wheezing Windbags and Bloody Busybodies

✳ A slippery genius on a nonstop trip around your body
✳ A cocktail of plasma, red and white blood cells, and platelets
✳ Brings essential supplies to your cells and whisks away the waste

Meet the Red Baron, the king of supply and demand! I run a collection and delivery service for the body, and whaddya know, it's one fluid operation.

The only time you see me is when you cut yourself, so many people don't like me. But there's nothing to be afraid of. I'm a transportation coordinator with three handy helpers onboard. Red Blood Cell carries oxygen around your body (making me scarlet with pride!). White Blood Cells battle against intruders, helped by tiny platelets. These clever fellows clot on contact with air to form hard, scabby barriers on your skin. Besides oxygen, I move nutrients, such as fats, proteins, carbohydrates, and essential minerals, all the way around your body. I even have a sideline in hormones! Truly amazing!

● Amount of blood in an average human body: approximately 10.5 pt. (5L)
● Makeup: 54.3% plasma; 45% RBC; 0.7% WBC
● Life span of a platelet: 8 to 12 days

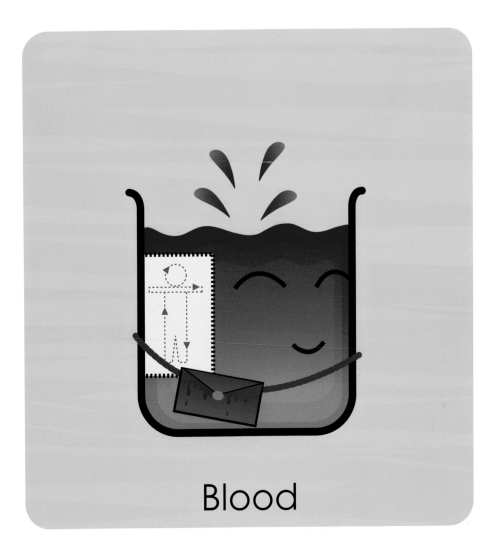

Blood

Lungs
■ Wheezing Windbags and Bloody Busybodies

* ✳ A pair of internal balloon heads who love to take the air
* ✳ These blood-soaked lobes are powered by your diaphragm
* ✳ Breathing is automatic but can be controlled consciously

Heave-ho! We are the bellow fellows, the inflatables in charge of your body's ventilation. It's a complex task, so take a deep breath—you're gonna need it!

We are two spongy bags made of minute bubble-shaped chambers of the softest, pinkest, foamiest flesh. These are called alveoli, and it is here that oxygen from the air gets exchanged for carbon dioxide. Here's how it works: your windpipe divides many times inside us, making millions of microscopic tubes that spread out to all of our alveoli. Capillary carries Blood through the alveoli, with Red Blood Cell onboard, who picks up the oxygen, ready for transportation to Cell. As he does this, he also deposits Cell's carbon-dioxide waste, which you breathe out before breathing in again. And so it continues.

● Lung capacity: 1.2–1.6 gal. (4.5–6L)
● Number of alveoli in the human lungs: around 300 million
● Number of breaths in a lifetime: about 500 million

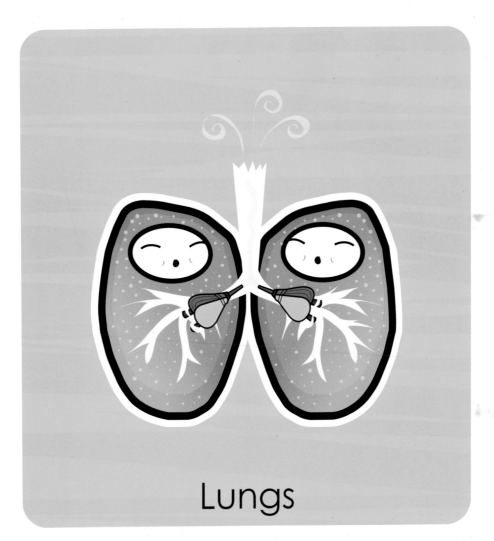

Lungs

Artery

Wheezing Windbags and Bloody Busybodies

✳ A set of pipes and tubes that carry blood away from the heart
✳ Forms your circulatory system, along with veins and capillaries
✳ Smaller arteries are called arterioles

You'll have heard that my buddy Blood uses a most sophisticated transportation network to travel around your body. Well, it's called your circulatory system, and I am very proud to announce, here and now, that I operate a large portion of it.

I run the main expressways that lead away from your heart. Mostly, my precious cargo is bright-red, oxygen-carrying blood. (The exception, my pulmonary branch line, delivers oxygen-poor blood to Lungs.) Pumped along my length by Heart, Blood is not exactly Mr. Speedy, but he *is* under tremendous pressure. That's why I need such thick meaty walls. You'll know if you cut or break my walls because I can spurt Blood across a room! It's a very draining experience.

● Size of main artery (aorta): 16 in. (40cm) long and 1 in. (25mm) wide
● Average width of an artery: 0.2 in. (5mm)
● Average thickness of an artery wall: 0.04 in. (1mm)

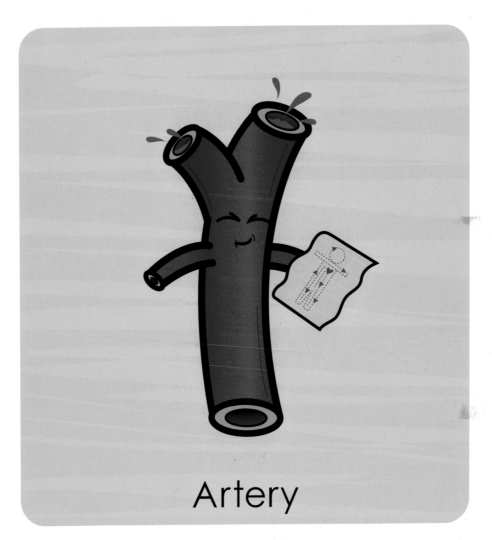

Artery

Capillary

Wheezing Windbags and Bloody Busybodies

* Micro blood vessels at the end of your branching blood system
* These skinny wrigglers connect to your arteries and veins
* These tubes refresh the parts that no others can

Tiny and oh so fragile, I thread my way through your body to feed it with life-giving, oxygen-bearing blood. I'm all over you like a rash, from the tips of your fiddlin' fingers to the tops of your twitchin' toes. It's through yours truly that Blood reaches Skin, so you can blame me for all your gushin' blushes. My tiny tubes break easily, which is why you bruise. Gee, I'm a delicate soul!

Capillary

* Size: 0.0002–0.0004 in. (0.005–0.01mm)
* Thickness of walls: 0.00004 in. (0.001mm)
* Typical length: 0.03 in. (0.7mm)

Vein

Wheezing Windbags and Bloody Busybodies

* This blue-blooded vessel completes your circulatory system
* Has valves to keep the flow going in only one direction
* Although it looks blue, oxygen-poor blood is a dull red color

Vein

I'm the body's aristocrat— a blue-blooded nobleman. I run the home stretch of your circulatory system, bringing woozy Blood back to Heart. Blood's oxygen-carrying journey is over for the time being, and who can blame him for having the blues? I may not have Artery's heartfelt pressure, but my one-way valves stop exhausted Blood from slipping back down the tube!

* Largest veins: superior and inferior vena cava (attached to the heart)
* Size: 1.2 in. (30mm) across
* Blood flow in vena cava: 0.04 in. (1mm) per second

CHAPTER 4
Food Crew and Trash Gang

Please raise your glass for the slurpy, sloppy stars in your food-processing factory—from pulverizing Teeth and liquidizing Saliva all the way down to churning Stomach and snaking Intestines—these guys operate your amazing digestive system. Working with a handful of deconstruction specialists, such as Enzymes and Gut Bacterium, these munchers get busy extracting nutrients to power your body and get rid of the stuff you no longer need. They're a noisy bunch—drooling and dribbling, burping and passing gas, as they guzzle their way through your food. But, hey, for them, life's just a gas!

Enzymes

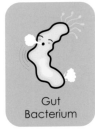

Saliva

Teeth

Stomach

Intestines

Smooth Muscle

Gut Bacterium

Gallbladder

Liver

Kidneys

Bladder

Waste Matter

Enzymes
■ Food Crew and Trash Gang

☀ Wonder proteins that are essential to your body chemistry
☀ Speed up chemical reactions, such as breaking down food
☀ Essential to body chemistry but remain unchanged in reactions

We are movers and shakers, real smashers that just make things happen. Scientists call us catalysts. That means we speed up your body's chemical reactions without getting used up or altered in the process. Smart, huh?

You can find different types of us all over your body. We're right on top of the thousands of chemical processes that occur. We make each one happen faster, while saving on energy. Who is it that divides your food into simple molecules for your body to use? Yep, it's us! And who helps make all those proteins that keep you alive? Right again! And because we are unaffected by the reactions we cause, we can repeat the job thousands of times a second. Without us, some of the processes would take so long that your life wouldn't be worth living. Ooh, feel that chemistry!

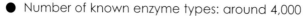

● Number of known enzyme types: around 4,000
● Digestive enzymes: made in the pancreas, salivary glands, stomach, intestines
● Systemic enzymes: found in blood, organs, and cells

Enzymes

Saliva

■ Food Crew and Trash Gang

✳ This slurpy drooler softens up food, making it easier to chew
✳ Contains mucus, which makes your saliva slimy and stringy
✳ The main enzyme in your saliva is a protein called amylase

Boy, oh boy, just smell that . . . aromas wafting from the kitchen always get me going. I'm a slippery, slobbery, slimy kind of dude who gets your mouth ready for eating. Ten to one, you drooooool every mealtime!

I'm liquid magic. I make your food mushy and easy to swallow. It's me that helps Tongue taste. I'm packed with Enzymes and get digestion going before food even reaches Stomach. I'm also stuffed full of bacteria. There are millions of these stinkballs in your mouth, which can mean only one thing: bad breath! I'm pumped out by six glands—two under your tongue, two beneath your jaw, and two under each ear. People tend to make a lot of me when they're excited, splattering friends with flecks when they talk. Please! Say it, don't spray it!

● Amount of saliva produced per day: 2–3 pt. (1–1.5L)
● Amount of saliva produced every month: 11 gal. (42L)
● Number of bacteria in your mouth: over 6 billion

Saliva

Teeth

■ Food Crew and Trash Gang

☀ A team of 32 smilers who grind and shred food
☀ These beauties are the hardest parts of your body
☀ Gunky plaque can rot your teeth if you don't brush them daily

Let's hear it for your pearly whites, your gnashers, your chompers. We're talking Teeth, and lots of 'em—your own personal set of grinning, grimacing grinders.

Say cheese and you'll show our handsome, heavy-duty crowns of enamel. Each has a root that slots into a socket in your jawbone and a soft center packed with blood and nerves. We work as a team. Frontman incisors bite and slice, while their spiky canine neighbors rip and tear. The heavies at the back—premolars and molars—chew, grind, and crunch their way through anything that's left. We may be tough, but we're not invincible. Mashed-up food and bacteria form a slimy, acid-producing coating called plaque. This can dissolve our protective enamel and give you a toothache. Ain't that the *trooth*!

● Number of teeth a person has: child, 20; adult, 32
● Thickness of a crown: 0.08 in. (2mm)
● Human bite force: 483 lb. per sq. in. (34kg per cm^2)

Teeth

Stomach
■ Food Crew and Trash Gang

* ✸ A football-shaped sack that mashes up your food
* ✸ Folds in Stomach's lining expand when you snarf a giant meal
* ✸ Produces gases that make wonderful, loud, smelly burps

Give me some food! Now! I'm one grub-loving guy, and there's nothing I like better than going to work on some tasty chow come mealtime. Burp!

I break down food into a nutritious mush called chyme before passing it on to Intestines. Sure, Teeth, Saliva, and Tongue all do a reasonable job up there in the mouth. But I'm a far superior being—a big, sloshing, gurgling, glugging vat of enzymes, bacteria, and food-dissolving acid. I have muscle, too, mercilessly squeezing and beating your nosh. And if I can't "stomach" something, I give it the old heave-ho with a swift contraction. Enough of your bloated boasting, I hear you say. Okay, okay! After about six hours of my churning, your food begins to look like thick pea soup. My work is done!

* ● Capacity of a resting stomach: 2–4 pt. (1–2L)
* ● Capacity of a full stomach: 8.5–10.5 pt. (4–5L)
* ● Time spent by food in the stomach: 3–6 hours

Stomach

Intestines

■ Food Crew and Trash Gang

- ✱ A 23–30-ft. (7–9-m)-long snaking tube inside your midriff
- ✱ Has two parts: the small intestine and the large intestine
- ✱ Fingerlike protrusions called villi increase surface area

I'm your body's food-processing and garbage-disposal plant. I suck all the juicy goodness from the mushy chyme that Stomach passes on. Waste not, want not!

It all starts in my upper part, the small intestine. I take bile from Liver and enzymes from Pancreas to mix everything up into a salty broth. My twists, turns, and hairpin bends are lined with little fingerlike villi. They wave around in the slop and the slime, soaking up proteins, minerals, vitamins, sugars, carbohydrates, and fats, which seep through my walls into Blood. What's left moves on to my gassy part— the large intestine—where I lap up remaining body salts, minerals, and water. There's precious little waste, I can tell you! In fact, all that's left at the end of the line are some squishy brown lumps headed straight for your bottom!

- ● Number of villi: around 5 million
- ● Time spent by food in small intestine: 2–4 hours
- ● Time spent by food in large intestine: 12–48 hours

Intestines

Smooth Muscle
■ Food Crew and Trash Gang

☀ Fine-textured muscle that works by slowly squeezing and pulsing
☀ Arranged in layers, with fibers running in a crosswise direction
☀ This smooth mover helps your stomach, intestines, and bladder

Sleek and sophisticated, I'm a real smooth operator. You'll find me in the darkest depths of your body, where I run an "insides" job for your digestive and urinary systems.

I am the smallest of the muscle brothers, and I'm also the most laid-back. While Cardiac Muscle works frantically to keep your heart beating, my action is very slow. My fibers are fine and delicate—unlike Skeletal Muscle's brawny sinew—and they contract in every direction. I work on my own initiative, scrunching up Intestines' pipes to help digest your food. My slow, pulsating movements ease your nosh through your body. You wouldn't even know I was there. And that's not all I do. I help push babies out during childbirth, and I squeeze your bladder to force out your pee—ah, that's a relief!

● Official name: visceral muscle
● Also known as involuntary muscle
● Length of muscle fibers: 0.008–0.02 in. (0.2–0.5mm)

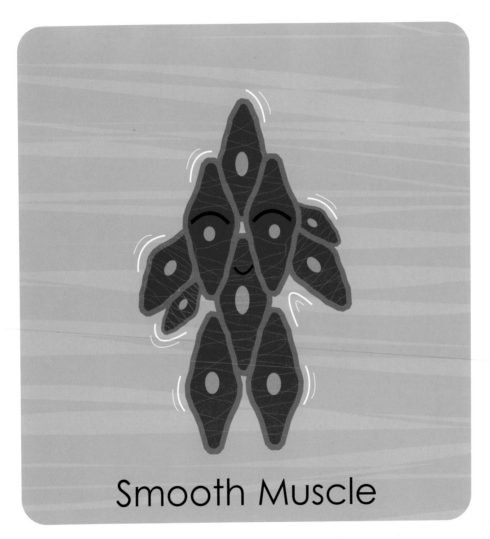

Smooth Muscle

Gut Bacterium
■ Food Crew and Trash Gang

※ Handy alien bug that wriggles and writhes in your intestines
※ Produces about 0.5 gal. (2L) of gas every day as burps and farts
※ Antibiotics can upset your stomach by killing this guy off

I'm a friendly type who likes to lurk in the glop and gloom of your digestive tract. I'm part of an entire alien ecosystem—trillions of single-celled bacterial lifeforms that call your body home. You have more of me inside you than you have cells in your body!

Thankfully, I'm extremely small, so you can carry me and my chums around without any extra effort. I may be a squatter, but boy, do you need me. Not only do I aid your digestion, but I also produce some essential vitamins and prevent harmful bacteria from gaining a foothold. Woe betide any filthy intruder that gets past Stomach's acid when hitching a ride on food and dirty fingers! Breaking down food is a smelly job—I generate a lot of gas in the process. I said I was friendly, but I never said I was pretty!

● Number of gut bacteria in a human being: 100 trillion
● Number of different species of gut bacteria: 300–1000
● Volume of bacteria in your poo: 60%

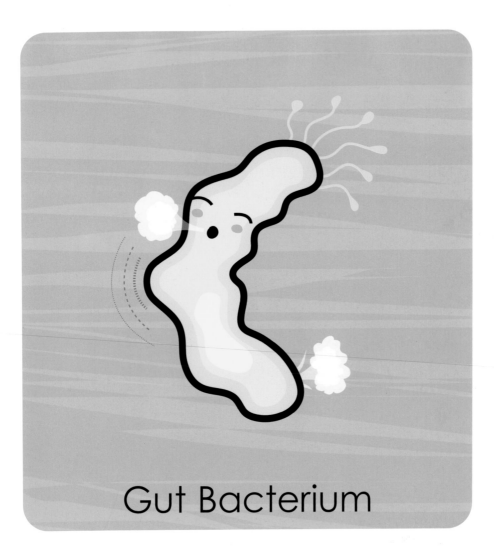

Gut Bacterium

Gallbladder
Food Crew and Trash Gang

✳ This old sourpuss stores bile in readiness to digest your food
✳ Bile is a gloppy digestive juice, the color of freshly cut grass
✳ In the gallbladder, bile becomes concentrated five times over

I am one glorious sac of bitterness in your midriff—a real bag of bile! In fact, my small pear-shaped tank is home to that very same acrid digestive fluid. You'll find me just below Liver, in a hollow crafted especially for me.

Bile is also known as gall, which is how I got my name. Liver makes the stuff, producing it even when it is not needed, so I get to store it. Bile goes into the vile mix that Intestines use to break down food. Mostly, bile dissolves the fatty parts, but it also helps absorb vitamins D, E, K, and A in your guts. My own personal moment of glory comes when Stomach releases its mushy chyme. I contract my sac, shooting my goods down to the small intestine. You might taste bile when you vomit. It's really foul and bitter. Some even say it's a "galling" experience!

● Size: 3 in. x 1.6 in. (8cm x 4cm)
● Capacity: 1.7 fl. oz. (50mL)
● Amount of bile produced by the liver: 2 pt. (1L) per day

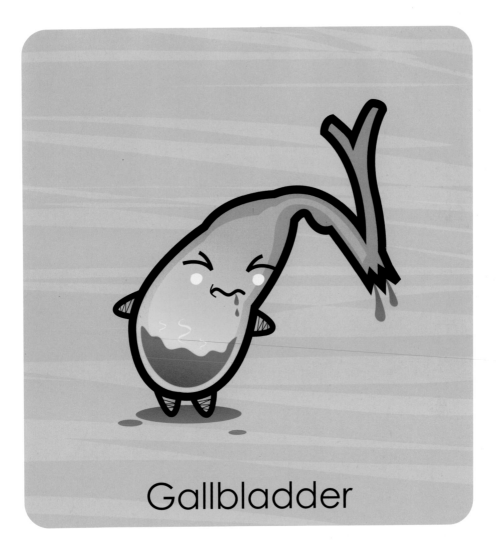

Gallbladder

Liver

■ Food Crew and Trash Gang

* A reddish-brown workhorse in the center of your body
* The body's heaviest internal organ, beating the brain to the title
* A yellowish tinge to the skin (jaundice) is a sign of liver disease

Wow! Is there *anything* I can't do? The most phenomenal organ in your body, I am a multitasker extraordinaire.

Just check this out! I'm a junkyard for proteins and worn-out red blood cells and a rehab unit that scrubs toxins from your blood. I send all my waste to Kidneys. But my specialty has got to be digestion. I process and collect nutrients from Blood, which gets piped into me from your guts. I'm a storehouse for vitamins, iron, and spare carbohydrates and fats. I make vitamin A and control Blood's sugar levels. I also produce gastric juices, called bile, for Intestines. Admit it, I'm pretty amazing, aren't I? It's a lot of work, and the heat generated by this powerhouse of activity keeps you nice and toasty. Hey, you can always rely on me to de-"liver"!

● Deepest side: 6 in. (15cm)
● Weight: about 3.3 lb. (1.5kg)
● Relative size of human liver: in children, 5% of body weight; in adults, 2.5%

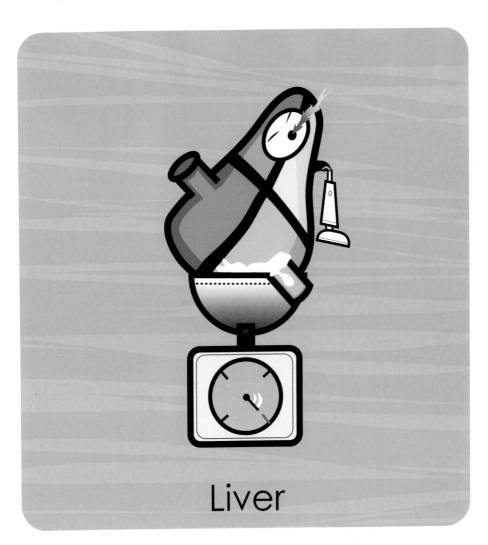

Liver

Kidneys
■ Food Crew and Trash Gang

✳ Dark-red, bean-shaped pair of organs in your back
✳ The main organs of your urinary system
✳ This dynamic duo filter blood and drain into your bladder

We're a couple of brazen guys who love, quite literally, to take the, um . . . urine . . . out of Blood. We clean up your bloodstream and pass all its waste substances and junk on to Bladder.

You'll find us nestled on either side of Spine, enjoying the protection of his bony ribs. Sure, we're kidders, but you could never accuse us of shirking. Over the course of any one day, we filter your blood about 25 times! Think about it—we spend our entire lives soaked in that red stuff. All the fun takes place in microscopic mini filters called nephrons. Each of us contains about one million of these guys. They squeeze water and waste out of tiny capillaries and whisk it away down garbage chutes to Bladder. *Bean* there, done that—it's our motto!

● Size: about 4 in. (11cm) high x 2 in. (6cm) wide x 1 in. (3cm) deep
● Weight: 5–5.3 oz. (140–150g) (male); 4.6–5 oz. (130–140g) (female)
● Total length of nephrons in a kidney: about 40 mi. (65km)

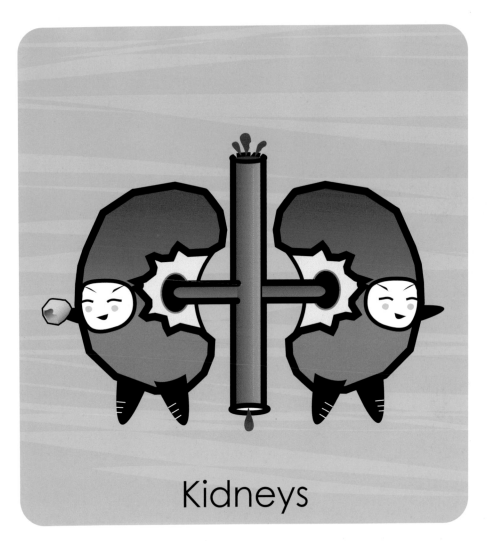

Kidneys

Bladder

■ Food Crew and Trash Gang

✸ This is the place where you store your pee
✸ Receives liquid waste filtered from the blood by your kidneys
✸ You have to learn to control your bladder as a toddler

I'm a pretty simple organ with a rather amazing talent. You see, I have an incredible capacity (get it?) to stretch and expand as I fill up with urine. No inflated egos here, I can assure you—I'm puffed up with purpose!

Each of your kidneys has a pipe, called a ureter, through which they feed me with the liquid waste taken from Blood. My outflow pipe, your urethra, leads away from me and out of your body, taking your pee with it. I have a direct line to Brain. Once I'm about half full of urine, you start to feel that familiar urge to pee. By the time I'm three-fourths full, Brain is well aware that you won't be able to hold on for much longer. Reach full capacity, and you've hit screaming desperation—you've just gotta go with the flow!

● Bladder capacity: 0.4–0.5 qt. (400–500mL) (adult)
● Length of ureter: 6–8 in. (15–20cm)
● Length of urethra: male, about 7 in. (18cm); female, 1.6 in. (4cm)

Bladder

Waste Matter

■ Food Crew and Trash Gang

✳ A stinky threesome who are always on the way out
✳ Straw-colored pee looks darker when there's less water in it
✳ Poo needs fiber in the diet to stop it from sticking in the gut

Two's company, three's a crowd . . . and in this case, not a crowd you want to hang out with! We are the toilet trio—urine, feces, and vomit—although you probably know us as pee, poo, and puke.

There's only one way food and drink gets into your body, but there are three ways it can come out! Wishy-washy urine is extracted from Blood by Kidneys—half a gallon (2L) a day! She's about 96 percent water and carries all of Cell's chemical waste and dead red blood cells. Stinky feces is a solid kind of guy, carrying those pieces of food that your body can't digest. He's jam-packed with bacteria, which is why he smells so yucky. Volatile vomit is more upchuck than waste. This is the food you get to see a second time when Stomach can't take it or has an infection.

● Number of toilet paper rolls used in a lifetime: about 4,240
● Lifetime amount of poo: approximately 6,316 lb. (2,865 kg)
● Urea: a chemical waste found in pee

Waste Matter

CHAPTER 5
Super Toughs

Get ready to pamper your body's beauty spots, for there's more to this crew than keeping up appearances. They might be good-looking, but your outer parts are also your body's first line of defense, and boy, do these guys take a beating with all the knocks and scrapes that you get them into! As well as the essential barrier services they provide, these dudes help you stay warm when it's cold and cool when it's hot. From Hair on your head to high-tech Sweat Gland and supersensitive Skin, this is one sophisticated, tough team that deserves a whole lotta praise.

Skin

Sweat Gland

Hair

Nails

Skin

■ Super Toughs

☀ This smooth beauty is your body's largest and heaviest organ
☀ Protects against scrapes and blocks germ invasions
☀ Controls temperature and interacts with the outside world

Silky smooth and supersophisticated, I'm your stretchy sidekick. I am the most high-tech piece of gear that your body has. A perfect fit, I am a temperature-controlling, hard-wearing, waterproof, and self-healing membrane.

And my beauty isn't just skin deep! I'm packed with hardware below the surface. In just one fingernail-size patch of me, you'll find a whole yard (1m) of blood vessels, a thousand touch-sensitive pressure pads, and a hundred oil glands to keep me nice and supple. In addition, there are micronerves, sweat glands, and hairs galore. I renew my cells in a cycle that replaces my outermost layer in about a month. This means that I shed about 10,000 skin flakes every minute. In fact, there's a sprinkling of dead skin on you right now—makes me tingle just thinking about it!

● Weight of adult human skin: 6.6–8.8 lb. (3–4kg)
● Average surface area: 20.5 sq. ft. (1.9m^2)
● Skin thickness: 0.04 in. (1mm) at birth; 0.08 in. (2mm) as an adult

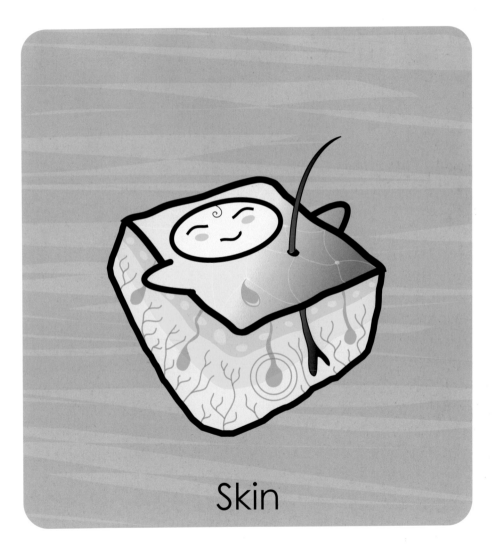

Skin

Sweat Gland
■ Super Toughs

- ✸ Slippery secretor lurking beneath your skin's surface
- ✸ This sporty jock makes sweat and pumps it out of tiny pores
- ✸ Works hardest when you get hot or emotional

Sweat it out, baby! Embedded in every inch of your glorious skin, I produce the juice that keeps your body temperature stable. I'm a cooling customer all right, and I just love a good workout!

I make sweat from Blood's watery part—plasma—which is what makes sweat taste salty. And I may make you clammy and red-faced at times, but don't sweat over it—I'm a pretty busy guy. As well as keeping you cool, I offer a fast track for getting toxins out of your body. I also squirt out antibacterial chemicals that keep Skin germ-free. So don't blame your body odor on me—I'm doing my best for you, smelly! On top of that, extra glands on your hands help you get a good hold of things without their slipping from your grasp. Gripping stuff, eh?

- ● Average number of sweat glands in a human being: 2 million
- ● Sweat produced on a hot day: 0.4 gal. (1.7L)
- ● Dangerous water loss through sweating: 5–10 % of body weight for a child

Sweat Gland

Hair
■ Super Toughs

- ☀ These woolly-headed fibers grow from roots in your skin
- ☀ Found everywhere except lips, palms of hands, and soles of feet
- ☀ The visible parts of hair are made of nonliving keratin

Let's not split hairs, now! There's nothing better than a thick, luxuriant covering of me. And I'm not just talking about your mop on top. Face it, I've got you covered!

I'm all over you. Ever get goose bumps when you're cold or scared? Well, that's me standing to attention, pushed up by tiny muscles in your skin. I offer protection (as eyelashes) and warmth (as scalp and body hair).

I'm a softy, but I'm also very tough—I'm made of the protein keratin and am stronger than a copper wire of the same thickness. I grow slowly and can reach 20–30 in. (50–80cm) long (as head hair) before falling out. That means your oldest hairs are three to five years old, and it's why you find so many in the drain! *Hair* today, gone tomorrow!

- ● Number of hairs on a human head: 130,000 (fair); 105,000 (dark)
- ● Number of hairs shed: about 100 per day
- ● Thickness of a scalp hair: 0.002 in. (0.05mm)

Hair

Nails
■ Super Toughs

✸ Little thugs found on your fingers and toes
✸ Made from flat plates of stiff keratin
✸ Never stop growing and in constant need of trimming

Hard as nails, we're the rough-bitten toughies hangin' off the ends of your fingers and toes. We pinch, scratch, gouge, prize, dig, and take the knocks that life deals us.

Our roots are our only living parts, buried in the meat of your fidgety digits, and we grow at a snail's pace. The parts you see are as dead as a dodo—flat, stiff plates made of the same stuff as Hair. Your fingers judge the hardness of something when you touch it, by pressing up against us. Without us, your rubbery fingertips would bend back on themselves (ouch!). We're good for tapping out annoying rhythms—oh yeah, we've got that nailed. And because we love to get our hands dirty, having a nibble on us is a great way to pick up nasty germs. It's nail-bitingly horrible!

● Speed of nail growth: 0.02 in. (0.5mm) per week
● Time it takes to replace a lost nail: finger, 4–6 months; toe, 12–18 months
● Longest nails: 24.6 ft. (7.51m) (Lee Redmond, U.S., grown 1979–2009)

Nails

CHAPTER 6
Nervous Numskulls

Crack open that hard head case of yours, toughie Skull, and you'll find soft, gooey Brain. It's a little like breaking the top off a soft-boiled egg and finding it mushy inside. But there's much more to this clever fellow, for he is the leader of a sparky gang of incredible senses. With the help of Nerve Cell and the coordinating genius of Brain's lieutenant, Spinal Cord, the Nervous Numskulls have the good sense to tell Brain what's happening inside and outside your body. It's thanks to these guys that the world you live in (and not the one in your head) looks, feels, sounds, smells, and tastes the way it does.

Brain

Spinal Cord

Eye

Ear

Touch

Nose

Tongue

Brain
Nervous Numskulls

- This bossy guy controls all your body's processes
- Made from yellowish gray matter and juicy white matter
- Can function for only 8–10 seconds without blood

Pea brain or egghead, I make you the person you are. I am the boss of your thoughts, memories, dreams, hopes, desires, and your mysterious sense of yourself. Wrinkled like a walnut, I'm not much to look at, but I rule!

My "head office" is divided into different departments. The brain stem is your life-support system. It controls automatic functions, such as breathing and digestion. The cerebellum is a mini brain in charge of balance and moving around. At my core, an egg-shaped thalamus processes information from my nervous numskull pals, while the hypothalamus is important in responses to cold, hunger, and pain. But my outer layer—the cerebral cortex—is the real brains of it all. It deals with all those smarty-pants functions, such as reading, writing, and speaking. Heady stuff, indeed!

- Weight: about 3 lb. (1.4 kg); or 10 oz. (283g) with all the water squeezed out
- Number of neurons in the brain: 50–100 billion
- Number of dreams in a lifetime: about 100,000

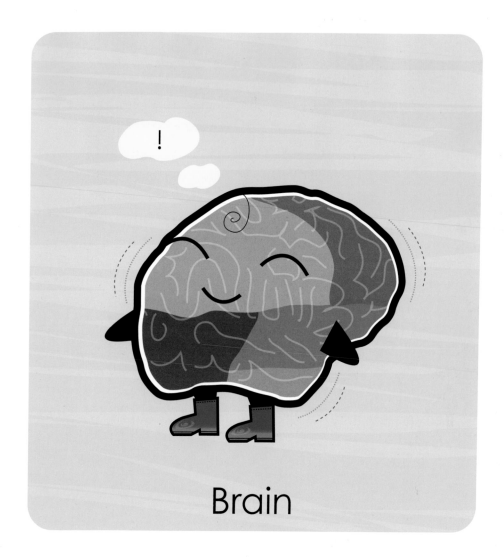

Brain

Spinal Cord
Nervous Numskulls

* A sparky communicator between your body and your brain
* Has nerve fibers branching out along its length
* Reaction times are fastest in young adults and slow with age

The king of speed, I'm a zippy-zappy dude who keeps you on your toes. I'm a slinky, slippery type who runs up the middle of your S-shaped spine. I am your body's information highway, and boy, I've got some nerve!

It's through me that Brain gets wind of what your senses are up to. Nerve signals whiz along my length like mini electric pulses and provide a high-speed link that warns of imminent danger. Quick as a flash, Brain sends an order to move, and I jolt your reflex reactions into life. This is how you can hit the brakes on your bike before you hit the wall. But I don't always need Brain to get you out of trouble. Say you're about to dip your fingers into boiling water. Well, it's me and me alone that makes you whip them out way before they burn. It's totally electrifying!

● Length: 17–17.7 in. (43–45cm)
● Number of neurons in spinal cord: 1 billion
● Typical reflex reaction time: 150–300 milliseconds

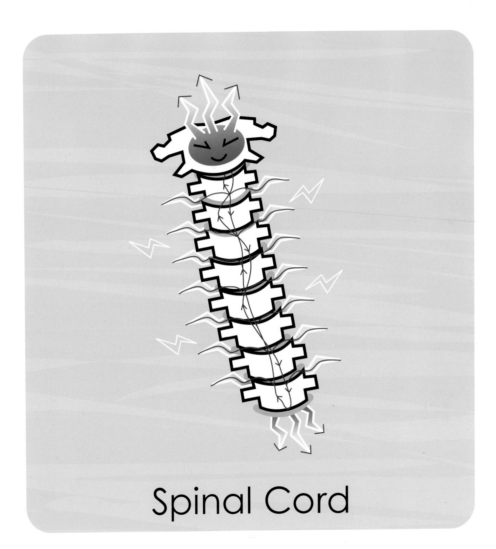

Spinal Cord

Eye

Nervous Numskulls

* A jelly-filled guy who gives you 3-D color vision
* Eyelids clean the surface using tears from ducts in the corners
* The human eye can see 100,000 to 10 million colors

Clap your eyes on me! I'm one eye-poppin' marvel that's gotta be seen to be believed! I am a true visionary who brings your world into glorious all-color focus. You can certainly rely on me to see the bigger picture!

I work a little like a camera, but there's more to me than point and shoot. Thanks to six dedicated muscles, I swivel around to look here and there (all the better to goggle you with!). My black center—your pupil—is actually a hole, and your pretty, colored iris is a muscle that I use to control the amount of light that comes in. A lens behind your iris focuses the light on my back wall—your retina—and, hey, presto, there's an upside-down image (well, nobody's perfect). Thankfully, Brain flips the image the right way up so you won't think that you're standing on your head!

* Eyeball size: 0.95 in. (24.2mm)
* Average time between blinks: 2.8 seconds
* Duration of a blink: 0.1–0.4 seconds

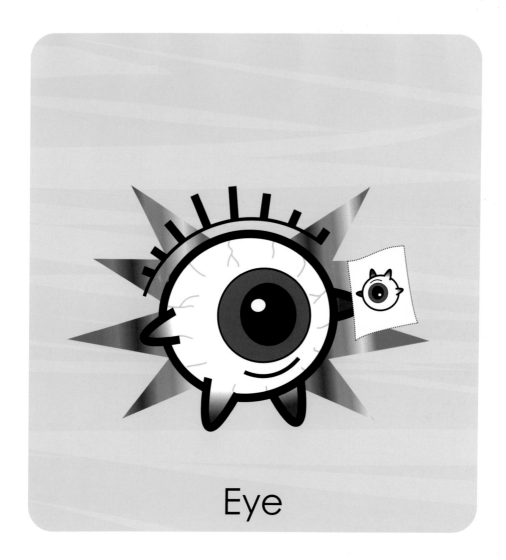

Eye

Ear

Nervous Numskulls

✴ Waxy guy whose good vibrations allow you to hear sound
✴ Picks up on both the direction and the distance of a sound
✴ Fluid-filled canals deep in your ears help you stay balanced

I'm all ears and completely wired for sound! You might think my flaps and folds and sticking-out parts look weird, but believe me, my strangest parts are deep inside. Listen up and I'll show you around.

When a sound gets made, my shell-like parts channel vibrations in the air into your ear hole. These beat a rhythm on my eardrum—a skin stretched tight over the hole—which in turn passes to the three smallest bones in your body: the malleus (hammer), incus (anvil), and stapes (stirrup). These rhythm lovers pass the sound on to the cochlea, a tube filled with fluid. Each vibration sends a ripple through the fluid, which makes microscopic hairs twitch and quiver. In doing so, they send nerve impulses to Brain, who interprets the signals as sound, giving you quite an earful!

● Smallest bone (stapes): 0.12 in. (3mm) long
● Number of hairs in the cochlea: 3,500 (inner hair cells); 12,000 (outer hair cells)
● Range of human hearing: 20 Hz to 20,000 Hz

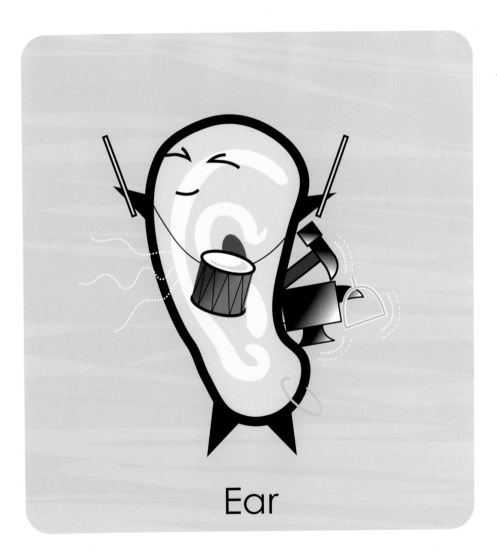

Ear

Touch
Nervous Numskulls

☀ Superdetector of pressure, temperature, texture, and moisture
☀ Pain sensors spread all over your skin warn you of danger
☀ Referred to by science whizzes as your somatosensory system

I'm "sense"-ational. Can't you just *feeeel* my vibes?
I work hand in hand with Skin and am spread out in a
network of complicated sensors, receptors, and triggers.
Come on, poke me! I'm all wriggles, tickles, and jiggles.

But I do have a serious side. Close to the surface of your
hairless parts are very sensitive sensors. They detect even
the lightest of touches and send early-warning messages
to Brain whenever you come too close to something
that might cause harm. I also have deeper-lying pressure
receptors that respond to heavy touch. These help you
figure out how hard an object is. It's because of these
little fellows that you know instinctively how much
pressure to use—or not—when holding something sturdy
(a rock) or something fragile (a kitten). How touching!

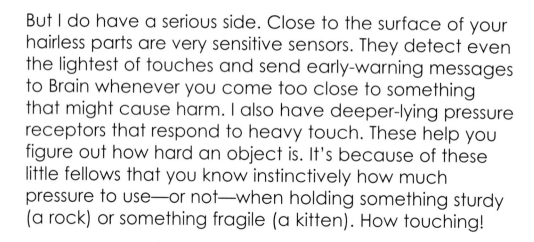

● Number of receptors in the human hand: 17,000
● Most sensitive areas: fingertips, lips, and tip of the tongue
● Least sensitive area: middle of the back

Touch

Nose
Nervous Numskulls

* Hoity-toity character with a famous sense of smell
* Gets your mouth watering before you even get food to your lips
* Your sense of smell is scientifically called olfaction

Schnozzle? Beak? What insults! Deep inside me (and out of the reach of exploring fingers) is a small patch of chemical sensors. Without these, you wouldn't be able to smell anything or taste your food. But that's not all I do. Tiny hairs snag grime on its way into your body. My mucus mops it up, and the hairs sweep the gunk to the back of the throat. "Snot" bad, eh?

Nose

- Wind speed of a sneeze: 100 ft. (30m) per second
- Number of smell receptors in a human nose: 12 million
- Number of smell receptors in a bloodhound dog's nose: 4 billion

Nervous Numskulls

* An acrobat with 16 separate muscles
* Helps you find your way around language
* Can get covered in smelly bacteria, giving you bad breath

Tongue

A man of taste, I tell Brain what's yummy or yucky when you eat. My surface is covered with thousands of lumps called taste buds. These little critters detect sweet, sour, salty, bitter, and umami (a savory meatiness) in your food. But, hey, there's more. Thanks to my muscular makeup, I can slurp food around your mouth and let you talk a mile a minute. There's no licking me!

● Number of taste buds on the tongue: 9,000
● Height of a taste bud: 0.002–0.004 in. (0.05–0.1mm)
● Number of receptors on each taste bud: 50–150

CHAPTER 7
Team Players and System Administrators

This little band of softies may leave a wet impression, but—respect, please—they don't have the most glamorous jobs. They drain out tired cells, mop up slop, and clean away toxins, poisons, and tiny living invaders. Someone has to do it, and like all service employees, these guys are pretty indispensible. Team Immunity fights infections and helps prevent future illnesses. These guys operate hand in hand with Lymph's incredible system to keep you spick-and-span. Unlike Heart, Lymph doesn't use a pump to get moving. Instead, the slippery stuff slides through tiny tubes powered by muscle contractions. Heave-ho!

Lymph

Team Immunity

Spleen

Hormones

Pancreas

Gland Gang

Lymph
■ Team Players and System Administrators

✳ Watery liquid with the same salty makeup as blood plasma
✳ Runs all around your body with Team Immunity onboard
✳ Has its own system of tubes but no heartlike pump

I'm pretty wet—a real drip, in fact! I'm the pale liquid that oozes out from cuts and pimples before they start to bleed. I slip and slide between your body tissues to provide a cleansing service for Cell.

I'm made up of water, blood plasma, and white blood cells. As Blood squeezes through Capillary, I filter out and enter my own lymphatic vessels. I trickle around your cells, whisking away waste and germs. Team Immunity comes along for the ride, looking to combat any invading bugs. My lymph nodes are like field hospitals, removing the bodies of those who fall as the battle rages. These bean-shaped lumps double in size and become sore to touch when you are fighting an illness. Job done, I drain back into your bloodstream in your chest. Drip, drip, drip . . .

● Amount of lymph in the body: 2–4 pt. (1–2L)
● Number of lymph nodes in the body: 500
● Lymph node size: 0.04 in.–0.8 in. (1–20mm)

Lymph

Team Immunity
Team Players and System Administrators

✴ White blood cell duo that keeps you sickness-free
✴ Produces antibodies that lock onto germs to neutralize them
✴ Gives you resistance—immunity—to bugs in the future

We're a highly trained special-operations team that tracks down invaders in your bloodstream. You know the kind: bacteria, nasty germs, viruses, and parasites—filth, all of 'em. Always on patrol, B Cell spots foreign bodies encountered in the past and marks them with his antibodies. Then Killer T Cell moves in to finish the job. "Immunity with impunity," that's our motto!

Team Immunity

● Different types of white blood cells (leukocytes) in your body: 5
● Scientific name for B and T cell: lymphocyte
● Healthy white blood cell count: 4 million to 11 million per 0.03 fl. oz. (1mL) of blood

Spleen

Team Players and System Administrators

- Soft, purple cleanup guy for your immune system
- A mass of lymphatic tissue, left of and below the diaphragm
- Plumbed into your bloodstream and your lymphatic system

Spleen

Emphatically lymphatic, I whisk away all the debris and decay that Team Immunity leaves in the wake of its destruction. I'm talking antibody-splurged parasites and toothless bacteria—not pretty! I sweep up old red blood cells while I'm at it. At the same time, I house half your body's monocytes—white blood cells that deal with infection. I've gotta be "spleen" to be believed!

- Size of adult spleen: 4 in. (11cm) long
- Weight of adult spleen: 5.3 oz. (150g)
- Position in body: betweeen 9th and 12th thoracic ribs

Hormones

Team Players and System Administrators

* Regulate your body processes and control growth
* Govern your emotions and can sometimes rage!
* Part of the endocrine system, along with the Gland Gang

A bustling bunch of errand boys, we are your body's chemical messengers. Released by Gland Gang, we whiz around your body activating, stimulating, and regulating all kinds of activities.

Need a little more zip in your heels? We know where to get it. Feeling the stress of a situation? We've got just the thing to help you cope. We get bad press from teenagers and pregnant women, getting blamed for their OTT behavior, but take a look at everything we do. We regulate your metabolism and manage your energy and your sleep patterns. We organize how you add extra cells to your body so that you grow, and we help you mature into an adult. There's so much going on, who can blame us for raging from time to time. It's all part of growing up!

● Number of different hormones in the body: 50–100
● Thyroid hormone: regulates metabolism
● Adrenaline: increases heart and respiratory rates

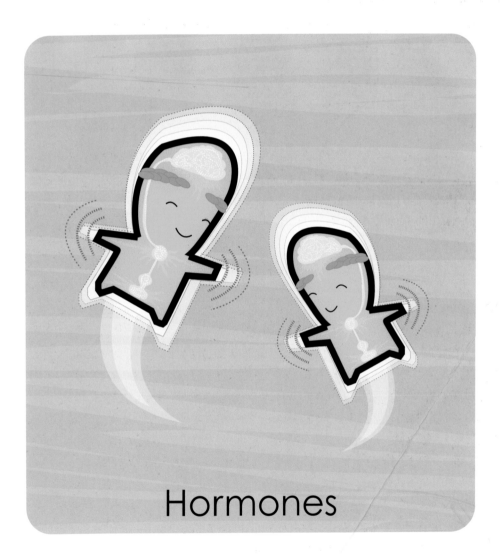

Hormones

Pancreas
■ Team Players and System Administrators

✳ Digestive organ that works in the shade of the mighty liver
✳ Produces digestive juices laced with corrosive chemicals
✳ Gland Gang member that produces insulin and glucagon

Slim and sock shaped (although without the holes and the stench), I am a factory for carbohydrate-mulching, protein-munching, and fat-guzzling enzymes.

My "hot sauce" pancreatic juices contain about 15 powerful chemicals that make quick work of your burger and fries. These juices are piped through my pancreatic ducts into Intestines' upper parts. Besides my digestive work, I have the important task of regulating your blood sugar levels: too high and Heart and Kidneys might suffer; too low and Brain could be starved of fuel. Enter insulin and glucagon, a balancing act of distinction. Insulin tells Liver to store excess sugar in your blood after eating, while glucagon gets Liver to release its stockpiles when levels are low. Gee, they're my hormone heroes!

● Weight: about 0.2 lb. (0.1kg)
● Length: about 6 in. (15cm)
● Amount of pancreatic juices produced: 3 pt. (1.5L) per day

Pancreas

Gland Gang
■ Team Players and System Administrators

✳ The floppy backbone of your endocrine system
✳ Produce hormones and pump them straight into your blood
✳ Pituitary runs the show, taking orders directly from your brain

We are a jolly bunch of squishy body parts. We might not be much to look at, but with *gland master* pituitary at the helm, we run a tight ship. Come and meet the team.

Tiny pineal is the size of a rice grain. Hidden deep inside Brain, this diminuitive genius controls your sleep-wake cycle with melatonin. Butterfly-shaped thyroid in your neck drives Cell to work faster and harder. Adrenal glands on top of Kidneys produce adrenaline when you're scared and cortisol when you're excited. You've already met Pancreas. Ovary (in girls) and testes (in boys) are the sources of your womanhood and manliness. Pituitary is amazing, producing hormones that control your growth while managing to run the entire operation. Shaped like a small bean, this little critter lives in your head.

● Pineal gland size: 0.2–0.3 in. (5–8mm)
● Thyroid gland weight: 0.4–1 oz. (10–30g)
● Number of important hormones: about 67

Gland Gang

INDEX

GLOSSARY

Amino acids These molecules are the building blocks of proteins. Your body produces 14 of the 22 amino acids it needs and takes the rest from food.

Antibodies Part of your immune system, these are produced by B cells to combat viruses and bacteria.

Circulatory system The network of arteries and veins that carries blood around your body. Also called the cardiovascular system.

Collagen Connective body tissue made up of protein. It can also be found in your muscles.

Diaphragm A sheet of muscle below your lungs. It contracts when you breathe in and relaxes when you breathe out.

Digestive system The body system involved in breaking down food.

Endocrine system A system of glands that produce hormones to control and regulate your metabolism.

Fertilization When a man's sperm combines with a woman's egg to create a new human being.

Genome The sum total of all your genes.

Gestation The period that a baby lives inside a pregnant female (35–40 weeks in humans).

Immune system The body system involved in resisting illness and infection.

Lymphatic system A network of ducts and vessels that transports lymph around your body.

Membrane A stretchy lining made from body tissue. Encases body parts and organs or forms a barrier between them.

Metabolism All the chemical reactions that need to happen to keep you alive. This includes reactions that build, maintain, and destroy your body's cells, as well as those that convert energy. Regulated by enzymes.

Mucus A slippery, slimy substance produced by the nose, stomach, lungs, and throat. It protects against, and washes away, irritants.

Muscular system The body system involved with movement.

GLOSSARY

Nervous system A network of nerves and neurons that transmits signals around your body and allows your brain to communicate with the rest of the body.

Nucleus The central part of a cell, where the DNA chromosomes are kept; a control center for cell chemistry.

Plasma The "watery" part of blood; yellowish colored and without red blood cells.

Platelets Cells without a nucleus; carried in the blood, they help it clot.

Reproductive system The parts of the human body that make sex cells and are involved in making babies.

Respiratory system The body system involved in breathing, centered on the lungs.

Skeletal system The system of tissues that forms a rigid framework for the body.

Water The number-one chemical in your body. It makes up 75 percent of a baby's body and 57 percent of an average male adult, and nothing could happen without it.